FIRST EXPERIENCES

DREW'S FIRST DANCE CLASS

by Katie Chanez
illustrated by Daniela Massironi

GRASSHOPPER

Tools for Parents & Teachers

Grasshopper Books enhance imagination and introduce the earliest readers to fiction with fun storylines and illustrations. The easy-to-read text supports early reading experiences with repetitive sentence patterns and sight words.

Before Reading

- Look at the cover illustration. What do readers see? What do they think the book will be about?
- Look at the picture glossary together. Sound out the words. Ask readers to identify the first letter of each vocabulary word.

During Reading

- "Walk" through the book with the reader. Discuss new or unfamiliar words. Sound them out together.
- Look at the pictures together. Point out any labels.

After Reading

- Review the picture glossary again. Ask readers to locate the words in the text.
- Ask the reader: How does Drew feel before his dance class? How does he feel during class? How do you know?

Grasshopper Books are published by Jump!
3500 American Blvd W, Suite 150
Bloomington, MN 55431
www.jumplibrary.com

Jump! is a division of FlutterBee Education Group.

Library of Congress Cataloging-in-Publication Data

Names: Chanez, Katie, author.
Massironi, Daniela, illustrator.
Title: Drew's first dance class / by Katie Chanez; illustrated by Daniela Massironi.
Description: Minneapolis, MN: Jump!, Inc., 2026.
Series: First experiences
Audience: Ages 3–6.
Identifiers: LCCN 2024044511 (print)
LCCN 2024044512 (ebook)
ISBN 9798892138703 (hardcover)
ISBN 9798892138710 (paperback)
ISBN 9798892138727 (ebook)
Subjects: CYAC: Emotions—Fiction. | Dance—Fiction.
LCGFT: Picture books.
Classification: LCC PZ7.1.C4794 Dr 2026 (print)
LCC PZ7.1.C4794 (ebook)
DDC [E] —dc23
LC record available at https://lccn.loc.gov/2024044511
LC ebook record available at https://lccn.loc.gov/2024044512

Editor: Alyssa Sorenson
Direction and Layout: Molly Ballanger
Illustrator: Daniela Massironi

Printed in the United States of America at Corporate Graphics in North Mankato, Minnesota.

Table of Contents

Step by Step

Today is my first dance class.

I am excited!

“Hi, Drew,” says Miss Maggie.
“Please line up.”

We stretch.

I have not done this before.

I feel nervous.

Miss Maggie does a dance step.

The other students follow.

I feel frozen.

Someone bumps into me!

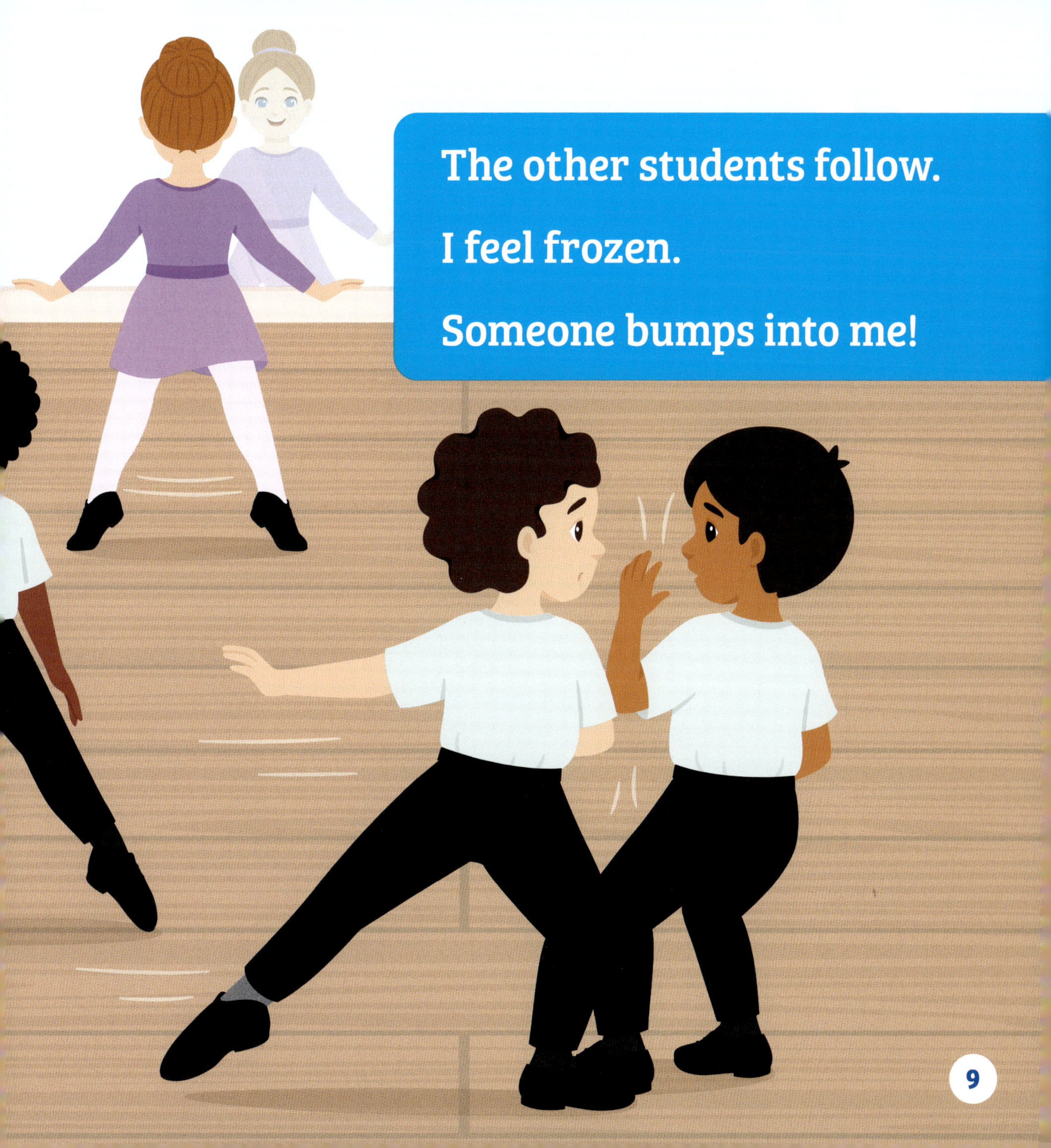

Next, we turn.

I slip.

I fall down.

I feel embarrassed.

My face gets hot.

"It is OK," says Miss Maggie.
"Let's try again."

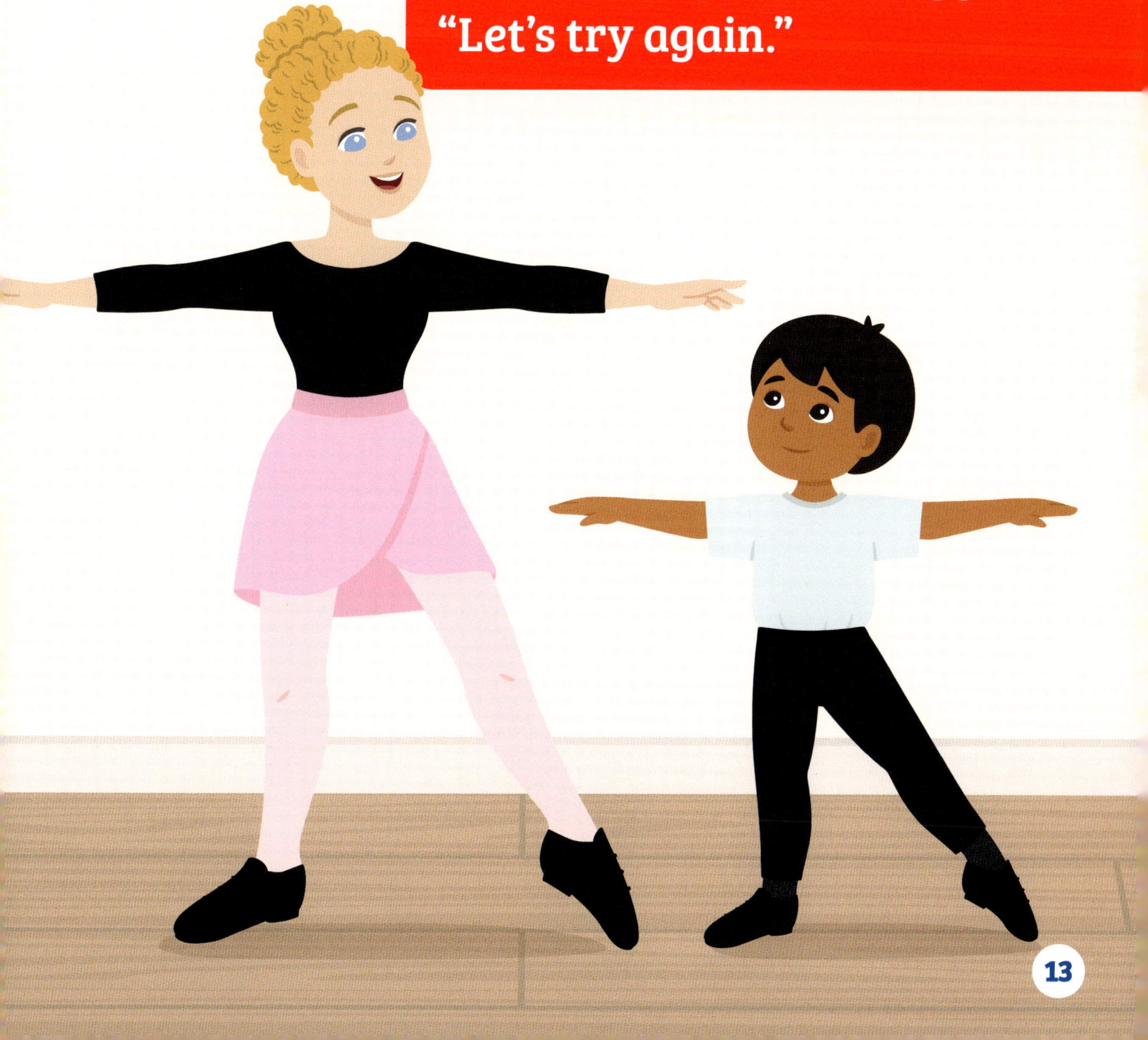

I take a deep breath.

I can do it!

Let's Review!

Drew felt embarrassed when he fell. How do we know this?

A. His face got hot.
B. He cried.
C. He left the class.
D. He yelled.

Picture Glossary

embarrassed
Uncomfortable and ashamed.

excited
Eager and interested.

frozen
Too scared to move.

nervous
Anxious or worried about something.

Let's Review! Answer Key: **A.** His face got hot.